EDGE
BOOKS™

ALL
ABOUT
DOGS

GREYHOUNDS

by Charlotte Wilcox

CAPSTONE PRESS
a capstone imprint

Edge Books are published by Capstone Press,
151 Good Counsel Drive, P.O. Box 669, Mankato, Minnesota 56002.
www.capstonepub.com

Library of Congress Cataloging-in-Publication Data
Wilcox, Charlotte.
 Greyhounds / by Charlotte Wilcox.
   p. cm.—(Edge books. All about dogs)
 Includes bibliographical references and index.
 Summary: "Describes the physical features, history, temperament, and care
of the Greyhound dog breed"—Provided by publisher.
 ISBN 978-1-4296-7713-4 (library binding)
 1. Greyhounds—Juvenile literature. I. Title.
 SF429.G8W564 2012
 636.753'4—dc22   2011011863

Editorial Credits
Erika L. Shores, editor; Sarah Bennett, designer; Marcie Spence, media researcher;
   Eric Manske, production specialist

Photo Credits
Alamy Images: Eye Ubiquitous, 28, Tomas Abad, 11; Bridgeman Art
Library: The British Sporting Art Trust, 12; Fiona Green Animal
Photography, 21, 25, 26, 27, 29; Getty Images, Inc.: DEA/G. Dagli Orti/
De Agostini, 9; iStockphoto Inc.: degeldog, 6, EcoPic, 17; Shutterstock:
EcoPrint, 5, 15, 19, Erik Lam, 1, Gelpi, 13, James Klotz, 22-23, Laila
Kazakevica, 18, Svetlana Valoueva, cover, Utekhina Anna, 10

Printed in the United States of America in Stevens Point, Wisconsin.
032011   006111WZF11

Table of Contents

CHAPTER 1

GALLOPING GREYHOUNDS

Greyhounds are the fastest dog **breed**. Their long legs and slender bodies help them travel at high speeds. Greyhounds can reach speeds of 45 miles (72 kilometers) per hour. In just three strides, Greyhounds can be running as fast as 30 miles (48 km) per hour.

Because they are the fastest dog breed, most racing dogs are Greyhounds. Each year, millions of people around the world attend dog races and place bets on the dogs. After Greyhounds retire from racing, many of them are adopted as pets.

breed—a certain kind of animal within an animal group; breed also means to mate and raise a certain kind of animal

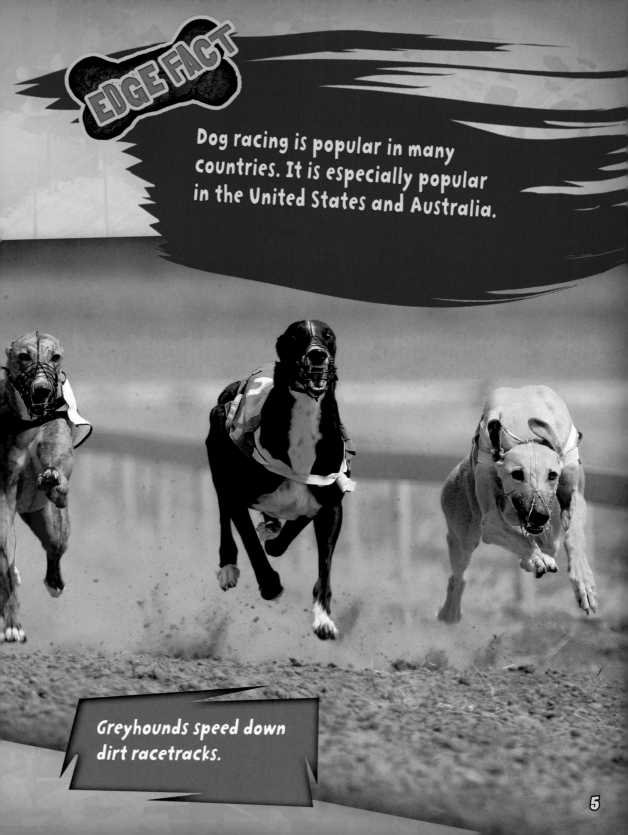

EDGE FACT

Dog racing is popular in many countries. It is especially popular in the United States and Australia.

Greyhounds speed down dirt racetracks.

Is a Greyhound Right for You?

Greyhounds are athletic dogs that need daily exercise. Most Greyhounds seem to enjoy chasing and running. Owners must keep them in a fenced yard or on a leash at all times.

Greyhounds should not live outdoors in a doghouse or kennel. They have thin coats and little body fat. These characteristics make them sensitive to cold, heat, and rain. Greyhounds should live indoors and wear sweaters if they go outside in cold weather.

In cold weather, dog sweaters keep Greyhounds warm.

Finding a Greyhound

Most Greyhounds in North America begin their lives as racing dogs. Dozens of Greyhound rescue groups work in North America. Group members get retired dogs at tracks. Some rescue groups operate adoption centers at the tracks. Other tracks provide information about how to adopt retired Greyhounds.

Most Greyhounds available for adoption are 2 to 5 years old. The 2-year-old dogs probably were poor racers or suffered injuries that prevented them from racing. The older dogs probably were talented racers. Retired racing dogs usually have some obedience training and are easy to housebreak. Most Greyhound adoptions cost $200 or less.

You also may adopt a Greyhound from a breeder. Breeders raise Greyhounds for sale. You can find a quality breeder through a local Greyhound club or organization.

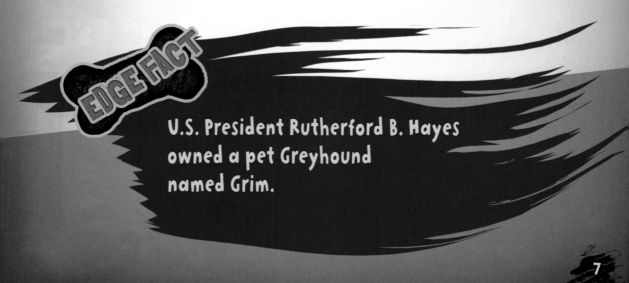

EDGE FACT

U.S. President Rutherford B. Hayes owned a pet Greyhound named Grim.

CHAPTER 2

GREYHOUND HISTORY

Greyhounds are part of a dog group called sighthounds or gazehounds. Breeds in this group hunt by sight more than smell. Other sighthound breeds include Afghans, Irish Wolfhounds, and Whippets. Sighthounds are long and lean. They also are fast runners.

No one is sure where sighthound breeds began. Sighthounds are among the world's oldest types of dog. Their appearance has changed little in thousands of years. Dogs with sleek bodies and heads appear in ancient drawings, statues, and writings from the region bordering the Mediterranean Sea.

Sighthounds may have originally lived in Egypt. Drawings of sighthounds appear on the walls of ancient Egyptian tombs built 3,500 years ago. The drawings show dogs hunting large game animals such as deer and antelopes. The dogs look much like modern Greyhounds.

Sighthounds appear in art from thousands of years ago.

EDGE FACT

The ancient Egyptians often drew the god Anubis in the form of a sighthound.

In about 600 BC, Romans from Italy conquered the Mediterranean region and ruled there for several hundred years. Egyptians, Arabs, Greeks, and Celts were some of the groups that lived in the region and kept sighthounds. The Romans took these dogs into their homes as pets. They called the dogs Celtic hounds.

Until about AD 117, Roman armies conquered much of Europe. They brought their sighthounds with them as they made their attacks. Many Europeans soon owned sighthounds. The English were the first people to call sighthounds Greyhounds.

EDGE FACT

No one knows exactly how the Greyhound got its name. Many people think the name came from the Old English word "grighund." This word means "hunting dog."

A Noble Sport

During the Middle Ages (about AD 500 to 1500), wealthy people of England's ruling class owned large farms. They often kept Greyhounds. It was illegal for working-class people to own Greyhounds. Noblemen hunted mostly for sport and used Greyhounds in **coursing** events they hosted at their homes. The dogs' hunting skills were valuable to these noblemen. By AD 1000, it was illegal to kill a Greyhound in parts of England.

At one time, only wealthy people were allowed to own Greyhounds.

coursing—the pursuit of running prey with dogs that follow by sight instead of scent

Coursing events became popular throughout England during the 1500s. The race area was called a course. It was about 3 miles (4.8 km) long. The rules were much the same as today's Greyhound coursing rules in England. People let **hares** loose at the beginning of the course. The dogs received points for speed and how well they controlled the movements of the hare. They received additional points for tripping, catching, or killing the hare.

In 1858 Greyhound owners formed the National Coursing Club of England. In 1882 the club required that dogs be registered. A dog could only race in public events if the club had its **pedigree** on file. Most of today's Greyhounds are descended from these early racing dogs.

Greyhounds displayed their hunting skills in coursing events.

Park Coursing and Track Racing

In 1876 Greyhound owners held two new types of dog-racing events in England. The first event was called a park course. This fenced-in course was 800 yards (732 meters) long. Its short length allowed more people to see the entire event. Dogs were judged on a point system similar to regular coursing.

The other event was track racing. Organizers set up a long, straight track. The dogs chased after a toy rabbit called a lure. But the dogs did not actually catch the moving toy. Dogs won based on how fast they chased the lure.

hare—an animal that looks like a large rabbit with long, strong back legs

pedigree—a list of an animal's ancestors

American Greyhounds

Greyhounds first came to North America with Spanish explorers in the 1500s. But Greyhounds were rare in North America until the mid-1800s. At this time, many people began moving to western areas of North America that were largely unsettled. In these wilderness areas, jackrabbits and coyotes damaged settlers' crops and killed their livestock. Greyhounds were good at hunting the unwanted animals.

In the late 1800s, Greyhound coursing began in North America. Owen Patrick Smith invented a mechanical lure in 1912. This motorized device moved in a circle around an oval track. Smith's invention marked the beginning of modern Greyhound track racing. Smith opened the first dog-racing track in 1919 in California. In 1926 the first dog-racing track opened in England. The sport then spread to Ireland and Australia.

The Greyhound racing that is popular today began in the early 1900s.

The American Kennel Club (AKC) accepted the Greyhound breed as a member of its hound group in 1885.

CHAPTER 3

BUiLT FOR SPEED

With their long legs and sleek bodies, Greyhounds are built for speed. Height is measured from the ground to the **withers**. The height of racing Greyhounds ranges from 25 to 30 inches (64 to 76 centimeters). Most racing males weigh between 65 and 85 pounds (30 and 39 kilograms). Most females weigh between 50 and 65 pounds (23 and 30 kg).

Some Greyhounds are raised only as pets or show dogs. Show Greyhounds usually are larger and less muscular than racing dogs. These Greyhounds also often have longer heads than racing Greyhounds do. The height of show Greyhounds ranges from 27 to 30 inches (69 to 76 cm). Males weigh between 65 and 70 pounds (30 and 32 kg). Females weigh between 60 and 65 pounds (27 and 30 kg).

withers—the tops of an animal's shoulders

A Greyhound's long legs and powerful muscles rocket it down the racetrack.

Colors

Greyhounds come in many colors. They can be black, white, or one of several shades of brown. They can also be light tan or dark red-brown. Many people are surprised to learn that few Greyhounds are gray. On a Greyhound, the solid color that appears to be gray is actually called blue. Greyhounds can even have color patterns. They can be streaked, spotted, or speckled.

Greyhounds can have one base coat color with patches of another color.

EDGE FACT

Greyhounds have good eyesight. They can see an animal move as far as 0.5 mile (0.8 km) away.

Bodies

Greyhounds' bodies seem perfectly built for running. Their **aerodynamic** body shape causes little wind resistance. Greyhounds also have long legs, a narrow head, a deep chest, and sloping ribs. A narrow head cuts through the air better than a square head does. Sloping ribs allow Greyhounds' lungs to expand and hold a great deal of air. This lung capacity gives Greyhounds good endurance.

The shape of Greyhounds' feet also helps them run fast. A Greyhound's foot often is called a "hare's foot." It is narrow and long like a rabbit's foot. Greyhounds have long, webbed toes. The long toes help Greyhounds grip the ground while running. The webbing between their toes provides more force as Greyhounds push off to run.

aerodynamic—**built to move easily through the air**

Temperament

Greyhounds are friendly dogs that seem to enjoy spending time with their families. Most adopted Greyhounds bond well with their new owners. The dogs usually are calm and quiet.

Some Greyhounds may not be good pets for families with other animals. Greyhounds have three levels of "prey drive." Responsible adoption groups tell potential owners about each Greyhound's prey drive before it is adopted. Dogs with a high drive cannot be trained to live with small animals. Most Greyhounds with a medium prey drive can be trained to live with cats and small dogs. Greyhounds with low prey drive usually have little interest in chasing cats or dogs. But people who adopt these Greyhounds still need to train the dogs not to play too roughly with the smaller animals. And even Greyhounds with low prey drive may chase after small animals outside.

EDGE FACT

Greyhounds have an instinct to chase anything that moves. This inborn ability makes them good at hunting rabbits and other fast game animals.

Greyhounds with low prey drive can get along with other pets.

Racing

Today about 55 Greyhound tracks host races in the United States. More than 25 million people attend these races each year. The length of Greyhound races varies. Tracks are one-fourth mile (0.4 km) long. Most races last about 30 seconds. The shortest race is five-sixteenths mile (0.5 km). The longest is nine-sixteenths mile (0.9 km).

Greyhounds wear special clothing and equipment when they race. They wear brightly colored blankets so they can be identified. They also wear muzzles. These mouth guards are used to identify which dog won if a race has a **photo finish**. Muzzles also protect dogs from nipping each other.

Greyhounds race for two or three years before retiring.

Racing Greyhounds are graded according to their ability and experience. They always race with other dogs of their grade. Dogs that win many races move to a higher grade. Race dog owners receive prize money if their dog wins. The prize money varies depending on the dog's grade.

Greyhounds race for two to three years before they retire. The top racers go back to their home farms. Their owners then use them for breeding. Owners hope that these dogs will pass on their racing abilities to their puppies.

photo finish—a very close end to a race, in which a photograph has to be studied to decide which racer has won

CHAPTER 4

CARING FOR A GREYHOUND

Greyhounds are easier to care for than some other breeds. But they still require grooming and exercise.

Feeding

Greyhounds are in racing condition when they leave the track. They may appear thin to their new owners. You can determine a Greyhound's proper weight by looking at its ribs. You should barely see the ribs toward the rear of the dog's body. Dogs are too thin if all the ribs are visible. Dogs are too heavy if owners cannot see any ribs. Greyhounds should not be overweight. This condition may cause serious health problems.

Greyhounds usually gain a few pounds after they are adopted. Most owners feed their Greyhounds 2 to 3 cups of dry kibble dog food twice per day. Kibble is good for Greyhounds' teeth and keeps their gums healthy. It is important not to feed dogs more than they need.

All dogs need plenty of fresh, clean water. They should have water available at all times.

Greyhounds should be fed twice each day.

Grooming

Greyhounds do not shed as much as most other breeds. Their short hair does not need much grooming. You should use a rubber brush or a specially-made coarse glove called a hound glove on your dog's coat. Brushing a few times a week or daily removes the dog's loose hairs.

Daily brushing keeps a Greyhound's coat healthy.

Greyhound owners should only bathe their dogs when they are dirty. Greyhounds' skin will become dry if they are bathed too often. The dry skin then will flake and the coat will have a dull, unhealthy appearance.

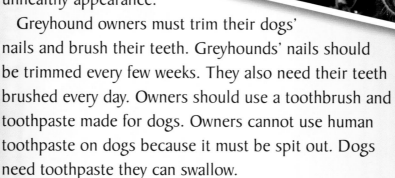

Greyhound owners must trim their dogs' nails and brush their teeth. Greyhounds' nails should be trimmed every few weeks. They also need their teeth brushed every day. Owners should use a toothbrush and toothpaste made for dogs. Owners cannot use human toothpaste on dogs because it must be spit out. Dogs need toothpaste they can swallow.

A Greyhound's ears are called "rose ears" because they curl back and look like roses. Because of its shape, this type of ear is not likely to develop ear diseases. But it is still important to check and clean your Greyhound's ears once a month. You should clean your dog's ears with a cotton ball moistened with a canine ear-cleaning solution.

EDGE FACT

You may use a bit of baby oil to clean your Greyhound's ears if a cleaning solution is unavailable.

Veterinary Care

Greyhounds need a checkup at least once a year to guard against diseases. At this medical exam, a veterinarian may give your dog **vaccinations**. The vet also will weigh your dog, listen to its heart, and take its temperature.

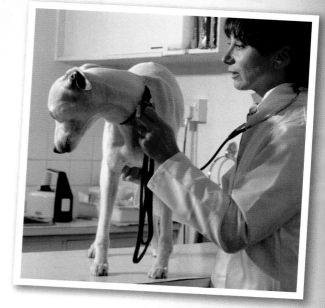

Vets also check dogs for heartworms and insects such as fleas, ticks, and mites. You may use a flea collar or apply medicine to your dog to keep these insects away.

Owners can give their dogs pills to protect them from heartworms. Mosquitoes carry the larvae of these worms that enter a dog's heart and slowly destroy it.

You should check your Greyhound's skin for ticks every day during warm weather. Some ticks carry Lyme disease. This illness can disable or kill an animal.

vaccination—a shot of medicine that protects animals from a disease

If you aren't breeding your Greyhound, you should have it spayed or neutered by a vet. These simple operations prevent dogs from having puppies. Fewer unwanted puppies help control the pet population. Spaying or neutering also reduces your dog's chances of getting certain diseases, including some types of cancer.

Regular visits to a vet are an important part of dog ownership. You and your vet can work together to help your Greyhound live a long, healthy life.

Greyhounds are calm, lovable pets.

EDGE FACT

Adopted Greyhounds usually live to be 12 to 14 years old.

Glossary

aerodynamic (air-oh-dye-NA-mik)—built to move easily through the air

breed (BREED)—a certain kind of animal within an animal group; breed also means to mate and raise a certain kind of animal

breeder (BREE-duhr)—someone who breeds and raises dogs or other animals

coursing (KORS-ing)—the pursuit of running prey with dogs that follow by sight instead of scent

endurance (en-DUR-enss)—the ability to keep doing an activity for long periods of time

hare (HAIR)—an animal that looks like a large rabbit with long, strong back legs

pedigree (PED-uh-gree)—a list of an animal's ancestors

photo finish (FOH-toh FIN-ish)—a very close end to a race, in which a photograph has to be studied to decide which racer has won

vaccination (vak-suh-NAY-shun)—a shot of medicine that protects animals from a disease

withers (WITH-urs)—the tops of an animal's shoulders; a dog's height is measured from the ground to the withers

Read More

Pritlove, Teresa. *Pet Dogs.* Nature's Children. Danbury, Conn.: Grolier, 2009.

Simon, Seymour. *Dogs.* New York: Smithsonian/Collins, 2009.

Wood, Selina. *Dog.* Owning a Pet. Mankato, Minn.: Sea-to-Sea Publications, 2008.

Internet Sites

FactHound offers a safe, fun way to find Internet sites related to this book. All of the sites on FactHound have been researched by our staff.

Here's all you do:

Visit *www.facthound.com*

Type in this code: 9781429677134

Check out projects, games and lots more at
www.capstonekids.com

Index